SUCCESS MASTERY

A Beginner's Guide to Mastering the
Inner Game, Do What You Love
Online, & Building a Digital Empire

E. Renee Williams

SUCCESS MASTERY

Library of Congress Control Number:

2024907493

ISBN 978-0-9834460-1-9

"Success is 5 percent strategy and 95 percent
mindset"

— Bob Proctor

Table of Contents

Introduction

Everybody wants success. Who wouldn't? Success, to many people, means having or achieving everything they've always wanted... and then some. For some people it means more money, freedom, power, influence, and recognition. Is this all there is to success? Of course not! So, what does success mean to you? Some people believe that success is the end result. It's not a goal, it's a process. So often when people have accomplished a goal that they viewed as the "ultimate success", they usually start to wonder, "Is this it?" In general, success is really about enjoying the journey that leads to the end result. It's about who you become and the challenges you overcome on the way to victory.

This book is about the mindset that creates success for new online entrepreneurs and the simple steps to building a thriving online business. Successful digital marketers don't move forward on their path recklessly. They develop the mindset that allows them to accomplish business goals and deal with roadblocks. Successful digital entrepreneurs achieve greatness because they know how to tap into their personal power. In this book, you will learn how to develop what I call "The Success Mindset"; this will give you the edge needed to get real results online. You'll learn specific ways of thinking and actionable strategies so you can start your business right.

The strategies in this book are designed to help you establish yourself and build momentum within the digital marketing business world through content and affiliate marketing. The key to digital marketing success is based mostly on your approach to the business overall. Even if you experience a few obstacles on your journey, the purpose of this book is to equip you with the game plan to overcome them in a powerful way. Let's get started!

1 Success On Your Terms

Success is not something that you experience by luck. It is something that you pursue diligently that is derived from a burning desire within you. If you are working on building your online business from scratch or you've already taken the first few steps to get started, it is possible for you to make it online. If you are willing to invest the time and energy into finding what really works, then you will experience success in your business.

Have you ever stopped to think of what your dream of having a successful online business means to you? So, what is it that causes some digital entrepreneurs to be successful and others to throw in the towel? Of course, any thriving online business requires you to find your audience, engage them, and deliver the right content, products, and services they want. However, it also means that you have the level of persistence and consistency you need in order to make it happen.

No one becomes successful by a sheer stroke of luck. Once you realize this, you will be empowered to create the life and business that you truly desire.

What is your definition of success? Once you have a clear definition of what success means for your business, you will be able to take a more strategic approach so you can go from where you are to where you want to be. Some people may not find it easy to define success. Any entrepreneur who has accomplished great things in their industry knew precisely what they wanted to do and who they wanted to become. They made sure that the time and energy they invested was doing things that were aligned with their ultimate goal. What is your definition of success? Some people may believe that success is associated with a title, symbols of status, popularity, or wealth. In an online business it could be the number of sales, size of your email list, or the impact you make through your ideas or talents. Sometimes success means taking the first steps toward making your dream of building a successful online business. Success is more of process than a final outcome. It is the process of taking consistent actions of applying your talents, passion, and ideas to accomplish your ultimate goal.

The pursuit of success means that you must step outside the box and allow yourself to become the person you need to be so you can achieve the things you truly desire. You are in the driver's seat. This is your moment.

> **""**
> Success is the process of taking consistent actions of applying your talents, passions, & ideas to accomplish your ultimate goal.

You don't have to allow circumstances to dictate your future. It's up to you to make it happen. Sadly, many of us adopt the generalized meaning of success that others may have for their life instead of finding what it truly means for ourselves. What beliefs, thoughts, or influences have shaped your idea of success? Do you feel that you are currently, or in the past, have worked towards someone else's definition of success?

It's important that you develop your own definition of success. You must be willing to invest in yourself and do the work in order to achieve the things in life you desire the most. Your success is the direct result of having an empowered mindset and taking consistent action.

Anyone who desires to be a successful entrepreneur has to know how to truly own their power. Owning your power means:

honoring your truth; being true to your vision, knowing that your thoughts and actions determine your outcomes, and accepting responsibility for your life. Success starts with you and that means you must eliminate excuses. Ask yourself, "What can I do to steer clear of a less than ideal situation?" "What can I do to get the outcome that I desire?" Doing this keeps you empowered so you can focus on things that will help you experience success. There is no way to have the level of success you desire if you only work towards it when you feel like it. However, when you take consistent action, you will be able to accomplish the things you envision for your life and business. Taking action means that you don't allow anything that has nothing to do with your goals to get in the way. You simply power through it. Complacency breeds mediocrity, action breeds massive success. Successful people don't allow immediate gratification to get in the way of their ultimate goals. You become a high achiever by taking deliberate and consistent action.

Your thinking has a lot to do with your outcomes. Unsuccessful people do not take the initiative to do what's needed for success because their thinking is based on failure or just getting by. It's easy for them to come up with reasons why things won't work out in their favor or reasons why they "can't" achieve something. A successful person will focus on opportunities and how they can make their dreams a reality. They have the courage to think big and consider what needs to be done to meet their goals.

If you want to achieve success on your own terms, you have to start owning your power in every aspect of your life. This is especially important regarding your business. In regards to business, it means removing all of the mental blocks, letting go of fears, and the thought patterns that cause self-doubt, and releasing the beliefs, circumstances, and relationships that no longer serve you. It's time to stop being hard on yourself and allowing "I can't" thinking to get in your way.

You must understand that by owning your power, you have the ability to take charge of your life and business. So often we get in our own way. We procrastinate and hold on to limiting beliefs. We fail to plan and allow ourselves to get bogged down by information overload and this prevents us from taking action.

Know for certain you can change your habits, thoughts, response, and your actions. You have the ability to control your thoughts. All of your thoughts, the words that you say and the actions you take must be aligned with your purpose, personal values, and your goals for yourself and your business. When you take control of these, you have the power to control your outcomes and achieve the success you deserve. Having a business means you must take risk.

Sometimes, when we know it's time to go to the next level in our business, it can be a little uncomfortable to take the first step.

We're afraid of failing or what others might say or think. We struggle with self-doubt and the labels that people have tried to attach to us. Then there are times when we feel like we've hit a plateau or feel that our dreams are so big that they seem out of reach.

Many people try to avoid taking the risk and they end up stuck in these negative feelings. This is where owning your power comes in with your business. You need to know that you have within you the power to create a highly profitable business and the life you really want. You have the power to make the choice to be stuck or take a chance on following your true pathway to success.

You can create the life you want and a thriving business. Your actions or inactions determine your outcomes. You must become aware of the decisions and actions you take according to the results you get. This is how you find out what works in your business. You need to take a closer look at the things you do on a daily basis. It's time to let go of excuses, "I can't" thinking, and all the things that get in the way of your success. The only way to success is to be honest with yourself.

Being an online entrepreneur is a highly sought after dream for many. In fact, about 72% of people have a desire to be in business. Starting and running a business may seem like a difficult challenge, but it's definitely rewarding.

There are a lot of reasons why so many people have a desire to be online entrepreneurs. **Freedom** is one of the biggest reasons many start their own business. You are empowered to shape your own destiny. It keeps you from feeling like you are in a rut and trapped in the daily grind. Having more **options** is another reason. You gain greater opportunities to explore new endeavors. You have the chance to do things that will allow you to create the lifestyle that you truly desire. Being able to make an **impact** is important to entrepreneurs. When you work for another company, it can be difficult for your voice to be heard amongst the crowd. Running your own business gives you the ability to make a direct impact through your unique talents and gifts. **Passion-** many people become entrepreneurs because they are deeply passionate about something. The chance to do something that you love and bring your ideas to life is a driving force that leads you to start your own business. You realize that the risk is worth it, because you know you have something of value to offer. **Vision**- You may have a compelling vison for your business. You are empowered to run the business the way you feel it should be run. Especially, if your goal is to help others and add value to your target audience; you structure your business in a way that will offer the products and services that your audience wants.

Authority- You are in the position to make the decisions that will lead to your ultimate goal. You prefer to be your own boss and take charge of your destiny.

Lifestyle- Being an entrepreneur can allow you to have the life you really want. It gives you the time you need to do the things you love in your free time. You can focus on your personal life, allowing you the freedom to spend time with family and friends.

Legacy- Building a legacy means a lot to you. Starting and running your own business provides a unique opportunity for you to do something that will give lasting meaning to many.

Achievement- Running your own business can help you accomplish meaningful goals that you have for your life. You may have certain things that you'd like to achieve and having an online business makes it so much easier to accomplish.

1 Success On Your Terms

What does it take to become a successful digital entrepreneur?

There are numerous benefits to being a digital entrepreneur, but sometimes it's not always an easy path to start your own business. You have to be willing to do the work and be determined. Successful entrepreneurs who get the results they want and are profitable online because they all have specific characteristics that bring them success. If you are determined to make your dreams of online success a reality, then you'll need to know what it takes to be a successful entrepreneur before you take those first steps.

The 7 Secrets of Highly Successful Online Entrepreneurs:

1. A crystal clear vision of the success they desire

2. A tremendous level of passion for what they do

3. Don't allow fear to hold them back

4. Belief in themselves and the value they offer

5. Are willing to take risk

6. Rise above both the "Status Quo" and social pressures

7. Have an epic level of determination

If you have the above characteristics or willing to do what it takes to develop them further, then you can be certain that you are able to achieve your dreams of having a successful online business. In addition to this, there are other traits that are important to your success.

Resiliency- At some point, every entrepreneur may experience some challenges or setbacks. You need to have the ability to bounce back and continue on your path.

Focus- Building an online empire requires a lot of focus. Successful marketers are able to stay laser focused on creating their ideal outcomes.

Growth- Anyone who has been successful online knows how important it is to continue learning and growing in knowledge of techniques they can implement to get phenomenal results in their business.

The key to achieving the success you desire is consistently developing your unique talents and allowing yourself to build on new skills so you can start your business right from day one.

The Truth About Making Money Online

I'm going to share a little secret with you. Now, this is the truth about making money online. Here it is...the reason that most people never make any money online is they're not willing to roll up their sleeves and do the work. Here's what I mean. Tons of people have been sold the idea of being able to make "money in their pajamas" or on autopilot with little effort by dozens of internet gurus. Many people think that all you have to do is press a few buttons, throw up a website, and watch the money roll in.

1 Success On Your Terms

Here's the truth— if you want to build a real business and make real profits, then it's going to require work. Too many people start only to give up after a short time because building a thriving online business is work. They go into it without a real vison, the wrong mindset, and without a real plan. This is what causes the overwhelm and frustration that causes many people to give up.

So, is it really possible to have the freedom, lifestyle, and income that having a successful online can give? It certainly is, if you have the right blueprint to guide you and you're willing to do a little work in the beginning so you can ultimately have the time and freedom you want to live the life you desire. Throughout this book I'm going to show you exactly what it takes to build a profitable online business. In the next chapter I'll explain how to create an extraordinary vision around what you're passionate about. In the following chapter I'll show you how to overcome the fear and roadblocks that hinder online business success.

2 Vision Is Essential

Now that you have defined success on your own terms, you must decide what you really want to accomplish in your business. What is it that you really want to achieve? What is the next level for your business? As you travel on your success pathway, it's important for you to have a vision of where you want to be.

Do you feel out of touch with your dreams? Have your priorities changed? Do you want to rekindle your business passion so you can build a business you love? One of the biggest reasons most people don't get the results they want in their online business is, they have not created a clear vision of what they truly want. We all have that special "something" within us that's unique and can propel us onto our true path. However, you might have had some well-meaning people, and maybe some that weren't, in your life who have tried to influence you to go in a direction that is not in harmony with your true desires. As time went by, you may have heard, "Can you really make money online?" Over the years, many people lose sight of what they really want and somewhere along the way started living their lives to make others happy. Many settle for the status quo only to end up miserable in what many consider a "real job" instead of becoming an entrepreneur.

In the process of "doing what's right", sometimes we get off track from our original dream. So what should you do to get back that burning desire you once had to be a successful entrepreneur? Simple, be honest with yourself about what you really want. If you want to be a successful entrepreneur, then you need to be crystal clear about what YOU want to accomplish.

One of the most common things I encounter when coaching people is, they think they cannot turn their passion into a profitable online business. There are so many ways to make money online, real money. Even if you want to bring your offline business online to get more leads sales. It is possible to make a living online with a business that you love. You simply need to make a decision on what you'd really like to achieve, and I will show you throughout each chapter of this book how online entrepreneurs achieve massive success.

In order to get your business to the level you've dreamed of, there is something you absolutely must do to reach this new level. You need a vision that is clear and compelling. Your vision will provide a detailed picture of your current state and where you want your business to be. Sometimes we get stuck on the "how". Right now your biggest priority is your destination.

As you go on this journey to entrepreneurial success, you begin to realize that as you focus on where you want to go the people, resources, and money you need will seem to fall into place. The more you stay focused on your vision, the clearer your path will become. As you move into the direction of your dreams, "how" or the next course of action or opportunity will come to you at just the right time.

> **❝❝**
> The more you stay
> focused on your vision,
> the more clear your
> path will become.

Don't put any limitations on your vison. There is nothing wrong with dreaming big. It's important for you to think about your dreams and your vision, knowing that it's possible. Your vision will help you layout the foundation for you to build your online success. Don't allow others to cloud your vision.

There may be some people you encounter who may try to discourage you or talk you out of your dream. Don't let it happen! In a later chapter, I go into detail on dealing with haters and naysayers. For now, I want you to know that your vision is the first building block to success. This book was created to help you develop your vision so you can move forward confidently in the direction of your dreams. In regards to business success, your vision gives you the ability to think about positive outcomes. The key is to set aside time each day to envision exactly where you want your business to be.

2 Vision Is Essential

Develop Your Passion

If you want your vision to be a reality, then you need to know that it's possible to turn your passion into a thriving online business. So how do you find and focus on what you are truly passionate about and turn that into an online business? Your expertise, gifts, and unique talents are revealed in the level of enthusiasm and specific interest that you have. These are things you truly enjoy. It's the things you are able to do with little to no effort or easily lose track of time whenever you're engaged in it. Your passion could also be revealed by things that resonate deeply with you. It brings out that special something within that drives you and gives you a feeling of fulfillment. When you are pursuing your passion new information is easier to learn and obstacles are easier to overcome.

When you are in the flow of your passion, it shows in every aspect of your business. It enables you to provide an outstanding level of value to your audience that will build a solid relationship and turn them into repeat buyers. Always choose a business idea that you love and can scale. If you don't have passion for it, you could easily lose sight of having a business that you love. The best way to make your business profitable is to incorporate your passion into your business. A lack of passion will cause you to give in, become burnt out, or throw in the towel when roadblocks come up. You need to be willing to push through and take risk even when it seems like you're getting nowhere.

The first few years of your online business are critical. Turning your passion into a business helps you build a foundation that makes it easier to transform it into a wildly successful endeavor. To reach your goal, you need a burning desire for it. The passion you have is based on that one thing you think about most of the time. It gives you the jumpstart you need to pursue your goals and do the work needed to make it happen. It's the driving force that makes you want to get up a little earlier or stay up late to get things done. You are willing to go the extra mile because you are committed to something you really love. As an online entrepreneur, passion is necessary for success. If you are not doing what you love, then you need to think about what your passions are and build a business based on it. So, how exactly do you find what you really love?

Here's a quick exercise that can help you pinpoint your passion so you can build a business you love.

1. If money and time were not an issue, what would you absolutely love to spend each day doing?

_____

_____

_____

_____

2. What experience or accomplishment you've had that's made a big impact or difference in your life?

_____

_____

_____

_____

Know Your "Why"

One of the best secrets to having a successful online business is to be crystal clear about why you're starting it. What do you want your life to be like a year or two from now? What is your ultimate goal and how will your online business get you where you want to be? Knowing the answer to these questions is what will keep you going, giving you the drive to stick with it. If you want to build a business that grows at a steady pace without getting overwhelmed, then it's important to understand your "why". Your reasons for being in business will help you maintain a positive perspective. Also, when you get into a routine sometimes it can be easy to get bored or distracted. Staying mindful of the reasons why you are in this to begin with will help you stay passionate. The last thing you want to do is lose interest and give up. All successful entrepreneurs who achieve massive success, are the ones who were determined to follow their dreams and had a compelling reason why they need to make it.

Ask yourself these questions.

1. Would you like to use your unique knowledge, experiences, or talents and build a profitable business doing what you love?

2. Do you want to have more time and flexibility to do things you enjoy? What would you do?

3. Are you ready to make a difference in the world or help others?

3 Winners Never Quit

Are you afraid of failure, or afraid of success? Are you reluctant to get started because you think you won't be able to finish? Are you afraid because you're not really sure where to start? Fear can stop you in your tracks— if you let it. It's not uncommon for aspiring digital entrepreneurs to get caught up in analyzing, researching, and only talking about starting their business instead of doing it. There are many reasons why this happens.

Online Business Fears

1. **Fear of failure:** Being caught up in the "what ifs". "What if it's a waste of time?", "What if I invest in it and it doesn't work?"

2. **Fear of getting started:** Not knowing what type of business you want or where to start.

3. **Fear of upsetting family and friends:** They might feel you're spending too much time or money on your business; the lack of supportiveness or criticizing you for wanting something different.

4. **Fear of not measuring up:** Read a couple of books or viewed a couple of webinars, but you're still hesitant. It sounds like something you want to do, but you don't think you have what it takes. Fears caused by personal setbacks or challenges.

These are just some of the things that keep people trapped in fear for years. Working through these fears in the beginning will get you far better results in your business.

Failure Isn't Fatal

There's not a single internet marketer who has been an overnight success. Believe it or not, some of the best in the industry have experienced a few setbacks. As you go on this journey to starting your digital empire, it's going to be important that you face your fears now before launching your dream. Any time you start something new or do something that may put you in the spotlight, there's going to be some fear. It's totally normal to feel that way. The good news is that you don't have to let that hold you back. If you do, fear will keep you from achieving your goals only to give up. There will be times you don't get the outcome you wanted— and that's okay. Continue pursuing your goal until you achieve it. Sometimes things can eventually turn out way better than you intended.

One thing I tell aspiring digital marketers is, don't be afraid to make a mistake. One of the reasons so many people get caught up in research and analyzing before they get started is the fact that they don't trust themselves. They simply think they don't have enough knowledge or what it takes to be successful. Here's the thing, you're never going to know unless you actually give it a shot. The fact that you're reading this book proves you have what it takes. Keep in mind, just because one method or idea didn't work the first time, doesn't mean you should call it quits. One of the interesting things about being a digital entrepreneur is finding what works and what doesn't. For instance, say you create an optin page that wasn't bringing in enough leads; you can always test it against a different version to find the one that converts.

That's just one reason why it's so important to examine any challenge you come across in your business. Consider what may have gone wrong and learn how to improve. The biggest advantage to this is that learning from mistakes will make you more profitable in the long run. You don't have to beat yourself up about it; just make some changes, create a new game plan, and keep going.

Conquer Perfectionism

Sometimes when people experience fear about following their business goals, perfectionism can creep in. Perfectionism holds you back because it creates an illusion of progress. If you try to wait until you have everything in place or just right, you'll never get your business launched. Start where you are with what you have. The sooner you can get things done, the sooner you can get your desired outcome. It doesn't mean you can be careless nor do a rush-job on business related task; it means you don't need to second guess yourself. Perfectionism will only keep you broke and discouraged.

Another common issue for aspiring digital entrepreneurs is focusing on the money too much. When you're worried about making the sale it, can come across as being too "salesy" or pushy.

> **❝**
>
> Perfectionism holds you back because it creates an illusion of progress.

Focus more on being able to create content, products, or the services you'll offer so your customers will gain the value out of it. Do this and ultimately you'll be making the money you desire. Aim for long-term success and you'll never go wrong. Yes, I know, you want your new business to make money and lots of it, right? Maybe you want to create a better lifestyle for you or your family. Maybe have a laptop lifestyle enabling you to live, work, and travel anywhere at any time. You know what? There's nothing wrong with that. I encourage you to make financial goals for yourself and your business. Here's the thing...people who focus solely on the money or "getting rich quick" are the most likely to crash and burn. They lose interest, burnout quickly, and end up broke chasing the next shiny object.

Like I've said earlier, you need to have a really compelling and strong "why" that keeps you going. You're going to have times when things fall flat and you're going to have times when you have success beyond your wildest dreams. In order to have a highly profitable business you must be willing to roll up your sleeves and do the work that gets you to that level. You've got to be willing to put in the time and effort; that takes commitment, consistency, and courage. Having the courage to make decisions in your business is essential. Fear and self-doubt will keep you from making decisions and taking action.

> **""**
> Fear and self-doubt
> will keep you from
> making decisions
> and taking action.

This only makes it ten times harder to achieve the success you desire. Indecision and inaction because of fear paralyzes you.

The biggest part of making decisions is being informed and having the right information so you can create goals that will lead to a thriving digital empire. It's important to work through your biggest fear so you can move beyond it and into success.

Here's a quick way to work it out.

1. Identify your fear(s)
2. Choose a way to confront it
3. Gather the right information
4. Make your final decision
5. Follow your action steps

This was a simple exercise to help you gain some clarity and deal with the fear that comes with being a new entrepreneur. It's one small step to overcoming overwhelm. In the next chapter I'll show you how to develop an unstoppable and motivated mindset.

4 The Success Mindset

There is a huge difference between people who start a business and a successful entrepreneur. Every day people start all kinds of businesses, but only some of them experience the level of success they desire. So, what sets them apart from all the others? Simple, it's their mindset. Only some people who start a business think like an entrepreneur. It's one thing to create a job that you call a business and it's another to pursue a business that you're actually passionate about and take seriously. This is especially true for digital entrepreneurs.

Removing Mental Blocks

Developing the entrepreneurial mind-set happens long before you create a website, attract buyers, or anything to start your digital business. It means taking into consideration everything you want to offer and knowing that you are fully capable of being affective in what you do. It also means removing the mental blocks to your success, like self-doubt or negative self-talk. You may have a ton of passion for what you want to do and be super talented, but you also need to believe in yourself. True confidence in your ability can help you take something you do as a hobby and turn it into a business. The things that you love to do or envision yourself doing can and will allow you to make a living, but also a difference. It's really important before you start building your digital empire that you have the right mind-set.

Being a successful digital entrepreneur requires work. Even though your passion and drive can make it seem effortless at times, you still need to be dedicated. Being a successful digital entrepreneur means you must be willing to do the work upfront so you can have a business that runs smoothly. It means you're willing to roll up your sleeves, create the content, develop your unique game plan, learn the right strategies, and implement it all so you can sit back and enjoy the laptop lifestyle. You must be willing to put yourself out there, be decisive, and maintain a strong belief in your business and yourself. However, that's hard to do if you're letting self-doubt creep in.

Many people who want to start an online business don't for several reasons:

- They have no idea where to start
- They wonder if it will work for them
- Doubting if they have what it takes
- Being intimidated by the technology
- Second guessing skills or ability
- Wondering if they're "good enough"
- Trouble imagining making money from their dream
- Thinking they're not worthy of success

Can you relate to any of the above mental blocks? If so, then there's something you need to know. You're not alone; we've all been there, including me! The first step in overcoming these obstacles is to know that you can create a shift in your thinking that can set you up for success.

Create a Winning Mindset

Your mindset is one of the most important aspects of your digital business. The way you approach it is going to have a major impact on your results. Your mindset will determine how you choose to deal with failure and bounce back. Are you willing to see them as a lesson and improve? The right mindset allows you to see the bigger picture and possibilities ahead.

Changing your mindset isn't hard. Understand that your thoughts are completely under your control. You don't have to allow yourself to drift into a pattern of negative self-talk, which leads to self-sabotage. Instead, become more aware of the direction of your thoughts. Ask yourself is this contributing to the goals or success I want? Delete it from your mind and focus on the things that will get you where you want to be. Affirm to yourself every day that you are working on your goals to create a successful online business. Focus on your strengths and make your first steps with confidence. The first step is hardest, but it'll be rewarding. Mental blocks often develop from previous experiences and other parts of our life (childhood, school, unhealthy relationships, disappointments, mistakes, work related issues, or negative influences).

The first step to overcoming them is to identify them:

What's one thing that has held you back from success?

_____

_____

_____

_____

How were you affected by this experience? (What do you feel/think about it?)

_____

_____

_____

_____

What did you learn from experiencing that event that will help you move forward?

_____

_____

_____

_____

At the end of the day, there are two paths you can choose from to overcome a mental block. The first is what I refer to as the Distressed Mindset. This is when you have a negative thought about something that's reinforced by self-doubt and negative self-talk. It will only leave you feeling discouraged and ready to give up before you give yourself a real chance. When you have a Success Mindset, you learn how to encourage yourself and focus on the milestones you're making on your journey. Commit to looking for things to be optimistic about on your business journey. The more you focus on celebrating your success, the more success you'll experience with each step you take.

> **“**
>
> When you have a Success Mindset, you learn how to encourage yourself and focus on the milestones you're making on your journey.

Make Success Your Reality

It's a truly amazing feeling to have something that you enjoy doing in your spare time and turn it into a profitable digital business. However, many aspiring entrepreneurs, despite their passion for what they do, view their business ideas as if it were just a hobby. Sometimes they have a hard time thinking of it as a real business that can make real money. It's important that you truly believe in yourself and your business. Get rid of the limiting beliefs that are keeping you from making your next move. The same amount of value you inject into your business is going to be communicated to your customers.

There are also times when people who are just starting out online are reluctant to invest in their business. They are afraid of putting money into it and try to do every single thing on a shoestring budget while they're already struggling to make ends meet. It's far-fetched to expect to build a business for free. Don't get me wrong, you don't have to go out and spend all that you have to follow your dream. You can start where you are with what you have and still create tremendous value. Successful entrepreneurs have a mindset of growth. They know that they must invest in their business so they can get a return on that investment. Essentially, it all comes down to releasing the fear of failure and believing in yourself. You don't have to get all the latest and greatest tools and resources you see all the big names and gurus are using. Never be afraid to start small and build on what you do. Too often, I see up and coming marketers who have the right tools available to get started, yet they'd continue to chase the next shiny object instead of investing in promoting themselves. Successful entrepreneurs engage in their business with thoughts of abundance instead of scarcity. Your mindset will set the tone for everything. Focus on building a solid foundation, growth, and creating the life and business you really desire.

5 Build Your Empire

Now that you know the importance of having a clear vision it's time to turn them into strategic goals. Your goals must be measurable, which means knowing the exact step or action, and when it should be completed. Learn to create a clearly detailed description of your goal.

The Power of Focus

One of the most important things you can do is write down your goals. Write goals that are realistic, yet challenge you enough to go further in your business. The best way to meet your goal is to continuously recall them. Review your goals at least three times every day; read them out loud when you have time to yourself. Allow the feelings of passion and excitement flow through you as you read your goals aloud. Sometimes it can be difficult for entrepreneurs growing their business online— especially internet marketers. It can seem hard for you to achieve your goals, find your niche, or even make the money to live the life of your dreams and make a difference in the lives of others.

Many of us encounter some obstacles along the way. Even to the point that some entrepreneurs give up at the first set back. Successful entrepreneurs see an obstacles as a lesson or an opportunity, and find a way to creatively overcome them. They are persistent because they have something that drives them to really crush it in online marketing.

> **❝**
> Successful entrepreneurs see an obstacle as a lesson or an opportunity and find a way to creatively overcome it.

The single most common thing that keeps so many digital entrepreneurs from experiencing success is shiny object syndrome. Too many get caught up in the numerous tools and marketing techniques. So much to the point they never stick with anything long enough to see what works. The power of focus will help you become better at online marketing. You must be willing to focus on one method long enough to see what truly works for your brand and amongst your audience. Focus on one method at a time. Give it 100% and measure the results that you get. Based on those results, determine your next move. Don't worry about multi-tasking; you don't have to be the best at everything all at once. Whatever project you're working on, give it your full focus. Your level of productivity will sky-rocket and you'll be amazed at how much you've accomplished. Keeping yourself busy or trying too many new tools and techniques at once only gives you the illusion that you're "hustling". Don't be fooled. Passion + Focused Action= Hustle.

Passion **+** Focused Action **=** Hustle

Focused action is all about
priorities and taking a balanced
approach to your goals.

If you can't focus on something, then
you need to check your passion. Make sure
that you are passionate about what you're
doing and that you're doing it for the right
reasons. Stay focused on your current task at
each stage and the "how" on making it happen will come to you. Yes, I know it seems
like you have a million ideas. Don't allow
yourself to get so caught up in all those ideas

that you're not implementing them. Ideas are great, but execution is what gets you results. I'm not telling you something that I don't know. I've been there! I know exactly what it feels like to have tons of brilliant ideas. I also know what it's like to bounce around from one idea to another. It's absolute crap! If you're not focused, then all those brilliant ideas are going to waste. Worst of all, they're not making you money. You want the money? Get focused!

Focus is crucial for new digital entrepreneurs. Your ability to focus on one task at a time and bringing it to successful completion can make or break you. It can mean the difference in being a Wantrepreneur and an Entrepreneur. Perseverance is what gets it done. So, how exactly are you supposed to stay focused without daily life keeping you distracted? Goals.

Goals Make You Unstoppable

The simplest way to build your digital empire is creating strategic goals for building your business. If you don't have a real game-plan, then you'll be extremely unhappy with your outcomes. You can't just fly by the seat of your pants in business. When you create attainable goals, both short and long-term, you set yourself up for achievement, giving you a huge boost of confidence to keep going. Anytime a setback occurs you'll recall all that you've accomplished and find the strength to keep going.

Here is the ultimate process for success mastery with goals:

1. **Write down your goals!** If becomes so much more than a dream once you write down your goals. Once you have them in front of you on paper it starts to become real. This allows you to not only become more focused, but you'll become aware of the opportunities and resources needed to move your business forward.

2. **State your goals in the present tense.** All you do is state your goal as if you've achieved it and it's currently true. When your mind experiences this gap of where you want to be and where you are, it goes to work for you to make it a reality. You will begin to attract the right resources and people to move you forward. Stating your goals as

"someday" or "I will" makes it seem out of reach. In the present tense you see it as something that's definitely attainable.

3. **Set goals that are positive.** Your goals need to be a statement of what you want; not what you don't want. Whatever you tell your mind to focus on is what will become your reality. You can only take action on what your mind envisions daily.

4. **Your goals need to be specific.** Being vague about what you want to achieve gets you nowhere. Being specific gives you clarity about the actions you need to take to make it happen.

5. **Goals need to be time-bound.** Having a clear time frame for completion allows you to stay on course. It gives you something to

aim for and helps you break it down into micro-steps.

6. **Your goals must be attainable.** You need to believe that you can achieve it. Set goals that challenge you, yet something that you can realistically experience.

Find Your Tribe

Setting yourself up for success through the power of effective goal setting is one of the most important things to do in your business. One of you primary goals is to find your target audience. The biggest mistake I see aspiring entrepreneurs make is trying to market to 'everybody'. I ask the question, "So, who does your business serve? Who is your product for?" "Oh, it's for everybody!"

Then they proceed to try and shove what they offer down the throats of any and every one who'll listen. They do this only to find out that "everyone" does not need or want what they offer. Knowing who you serve and their unique needs allows you to stand out more and provide real value. One of the first things you must do as a digital marketer is getting to know your audience. Take the time to learn about the problems, challenges, and desires of your target audience.

Irresistible Offers + Right People = Digital Profits $$$$

Doing so will help your offers become irresistible to the right people. It allows you to use your resources wisely when promoting yourself online. You'll be able to present your offers in such a way that will make it seem like effortless success and music to the ears of your tribe. Knowing who you serve and what they need most, helps you to establish yourself as an expert in your niche. As a new digital marketer, it helps you validate an idea before putting all of your time and money into a new venture. Nobody wants to invest their time and energy into a business that will fall flat. This is a crucial step in your success. Understanding your audience allows you to set yourself apart from others. How will you serve them in a unique way? Once you've found your tribe, you need to build a rock solid relationship with them. If they are going to buy from you, they need to trust you. Remember everything I said earlier about making sure your business is something you're passionate about?

5 Build Your Empire

Here is where that all starts to come into play. Here's the deal...people know a fake when they see one. If you're only in this for the money and lifestyle, they'll know it. However, if you actually love what you do and getting people the results they desire, it will certainly shine through in your business. You won't come off as sleazy, salesy, or slimy. Whew, try saying that three times! You also build trust by keeping your promises. Simply be a person of your word. For instance, if you promise not to spam your audience on your optin pages, then follow through on that. There's nothing wrong with promoting your offer, but take a balanced approach with content and offers in your marketing. You don't want your tribe to feel like they've been duped into an endless pitch. You're actually here to help them. Keep this as your primary goal and you'll be well on your way to building your digital empire.

6 Haters, Critics, & Dream Killers

"Hold on just a minute. So, you mean to tell me that you're going to quit a stable job to do this online thing? Ha! Okay, if you say so. Let me know when you wake up from this dream and get back to reality"

- Random Hater/ Critic/ Dream killer

Ever experience anyone give you a verbal gut punch like that? The journey of an entrepreneur is not always easy, especially if you pursue something outside of the box like an online business. The journey can be even harder if you have to deal with unsupportive people. Despite the fact that so many people are finding success online, there are still some who don't think it's a legitimate business. Then there are some who dismiss the idea of starting any type of business altogether. So, who are they? They're the ones who chime in with negative comments, laughter, or ridicule.

Some people can be very cruel when they know you're embarking on your dream business. Some claim it's out of concern; others are simply happy to trample on your dreams. One of the many things you'll hear is that your goals are "unrealistic". Another is usually "you should just get a 'real' job." Don't get me wrong, I'm definitely not telling you to quit your 'day job' to start your business. Be smart about it. Work on building your business in your down time until you're earning a steady income from it and savings tucked away. Then make the transition from job to business or pursue it as a profitable side hustle. In regards to the haters, occasionally you'll come across people who react to your goals or business in a truly vicious manner— they completely ignore what you do or accomplish. Now this isn't too bad. However, when they are dismissive of your business or goals yet are supportive of others and throw it in your face. That's just toxic behavior. Yes, it can get pretty ugly! The biggest issue an aspiring entrepreneur faces is the critics in their life, most of the time it's easy to ignore. You can easily dust yourself off and keep going. This can prove to be a challenge when the worst ones are the people closest to you, friends or family.

For some entrepreneurs, the early days of building your dream is when the ugly side of people they care for emerges. I don't share this with you to deter you, only to help you be mindful of this on your journey. When the people closest to you are unsupportive of your goals it can be shocking at first. It may even feel like a knife in the back. I believe it is important to share this reality of the entrepreneur's journey so you can understand why it happens and how to effectively deal with it. Too often, aspiring entrepreneurs let their dreams die because of the negativity they encounter.

Why They Hate

Many new entrepreneurs often wonder why they encounter so much negativity. There are several reasons why some of the people around you are unsupportive. One reason is the fact that they may have had their own dreams at some point. For them, seeing you boldly pursue yours stirs up feelings of regret. It could be a constant reminder of the things they wanted to achieve. It's a horrible feeling to look back over your life and consider all the things you could've done. It's not an easy experience for them. It's definitely not your fault. At the end of the day everyone is responsible for the choices they make. Sometimes they can project their fears onto you. Everyone doesn't have the desire to step out and start a business. Some do, but may have a fear of failure, just not being "good enough", or deserving of success. Often, their insecurities and fears are aimed at you.

Despite your level of courage and commitment, they view your actions through a lens of doom and gloom.

> **❝**
> The most important thing for you to remember is to not allow the negative thinking or words of others to become a roadblock to your business goals.

People around you who've 'played it safe' all their lives and believe only in working a "real job" simply don't understand what it truly takes to be an entrepreneur. They don't realize that the people they consider an "overnight success" may have taken a few years to happen. Anyone who's achieved success in business can confirm this as a fact. The naysayers will criticize things they don't understand. Another reason people might hate on your endeavors is the fact that misery loves company. They've settled for where they currently are, believe there is no way to change their situation, or they're not willing to do the work to get what they want. The most important thing for you to remember is to not allow the negative thinking or words of others to become a roadblock to your business goals.

Dealing with the Haters

You may or may not have to deal with many people who'll trample on your dreams. I hope that you have supportive and caring people in your life who want to see you succeed. However, if you do encounter this type of behavior from people in your life, then I want you to know how to effectively deal with it. If you've already shared your endeavors with people you may simply need to ignore their negative comments. Just tune it out. If they say something to you, let them know you understand their 'concerns' or thank them for their opinion. Don't internalize or dwell on what they say. Put it completely out of your mind and most importantly move forward with your goals.

Don't worry about getting into a debate or even an argument. Don't worry about trying to win them over. Something you must do is to consider the source of these concerns or comments. Ask yourself, 'do they have any success in the thing you're pursuing?' Are they currently living the type of lifestyle you want? If not, simply let it go. Focus on building your business.

There may be situations where you'll need to distance yourself from people who offer nothing but a constant barrage of negativity. You have the power to choose who you surround yourself with and yes that includes family. Just because someone is related to you, does not mean they have the right to be nasty and toxic towards you. Set some clear boundaries for yourself. You can't achieve your goals if you constantly have to deal with someone berating or belittling you. Never allow anyone to make you feel small or stay in an environment where people are trying to hold you back. Limit your contact with them. You know your situation; only you can determine if its best to walk away, limit contact, or simply ignore them.

One of the best things you can do to deal with these dream killers is to make your moves in silence. Keep it to yourself! Many years ago I read a book about goal setting. Man, I wish I could remember the name of it. It gave one particular piece of the absolute worst advice ever!!! "Tell everybody about your goal", horrible advice. Can you guess what happened when I did this? I certainly didn't get the accountability and support it claimed I would. However, I did experience ridicule, doubt, and passive aggressive behavior. Stay quiet about your goals and let your results and success speak for you. Again, do the work and stay focused on building your business. Don't allow the naysayers the opportunity to steal your joy. You're not pursuing this for them; this is for the people your business serves. You're doing this to fulfill your life purpose.

7 The Road To Success

Many people become entrepreneurs because they were miserable with what they were previously doing with their life; some people come up with a unique idea. They were inspired and driven to do something they enjoy. The ones who become successful are the ones who know how to stay motivated. While quotes, books, programs, and events can be powerful tools to help you get motivated, there's an important key to staying motivated. Your mindset is the key to achieving real success. Having the right mindset requires you to shift your mind into the right state. Learning how to 'reset' yourself mentally and physically will position you for success. Your state of mind is affected by your emotions and physiology. It determines whether you have a positive or negative experience. If you want to stay motivated in your business master your mindset by managing your state of mind. For instance, you want to get your first thousand email subscribers, but you're sitting slumped over your laptop, allowing yourself to feel doubtful, worried, or fearful about whether this will work for you.

As a result, over time you end up being discouraged, lose motivation, and give up. By learning to control your state, you'll create a shift that breeds success. You need to speak and act as if you already achieved it. Your self-talk influences your beliefs. If you want to build a list, tell yourself that you're a successful digital marketer with a highly responsive email list that keeps your business profitable; conduct yourself as one also.

> 66
> You take actions based
> on your thoughts, emotions,
> and beliefs.

You must do this with a positive state; let yourself feel the passion and fulfillment of having the joy, freedom, and success you desire. Sit up; correct your posture as a person who is confident and successful. Hear me out; don't be dismissive of this at all. You take action based on your thoughts, emotions, and beliefs. To stay motivated you must begin by knowing that you have what it takes to keep going. Feel the positive emotions of having a successful online business. You'll have a high level of enthusiasm by allowing yourself to feel positive about everything you do in your digital marketing business. You'll be able to use this enthusiasm or 'peak state' to stay motivated so you can keep going.

Business Spark

The key to vitality in business is being in the moment and having the ability to see things from a new perspective. Don't beat yourself up over previous mistakes, or perceived failures. Don't worry about what's to come or allow your mind to anticipate failure. Simply be in the moment. Ask yourself, "What can I do in this moment to get my business going?" What can I do in this moment to launch my website, create my product, or build my list?" Here's the absolute truth, once you realize you have power over your thoughts, you can direct them in such a way to build your success. When you are mindful of the fact that everything you do each day is a building block to success, you'll begin to see your progress. The moment you see the progress, it'll give your business that spark. When you are focused and present in each of your business task, you gain a better understanding of how all the different parts fit together. This enables you to clearly see the big picture and stay on course to building your digital empire. This will also empower you to stick to methods without worrying whether or not it will work for you. Within the internet marketing industry, you must be willing and able to do some real work up-front so you can build a streamlined system that makes you money and gives you the time and freedom you desire. Websites and landing pages don't build themselves. Auto-responders, blog post, sales pages, and ebooks don't write themselves. Can you outsource some of these? Sure, but most entrepreneurs who aren't just in this to make a quick buck want to be immersed in their content and work. Don't get me wrong, if you need to outsource certain task, by all means do so. Everyone can't be their own graphic designer or write copy for websites. The point I'm driving home is this, be present or in the moment of your business task. Inject who you are into what you do in each moment. The sense of fulfillment you get will propel you and keep you going on a daily basis. People are anxiously waiting for the value you have to offer.

The Greatest Motivation

So what is it that really keeps you going, producing results? Positive feedback from the people you serve is great. It's really cool when people compliment you on your work. However, the greatest motivation of all is knowing that you'll have an impact on others. How do you determine if you're having a great impact on others? Become more engaged with your audience. You can do this through the content you create on your website, blog comments, emails, social media, and videos. Create a sense of community amongst your people. Communication is the key to achieving this. One of the easiest ways is video marketing. This gives you one of the best methods of engaging with your content. The secret is to produce content that is relevant to your audience. This is true with any method that's utilized in your digital marketing. If you're going to help your audience get results, you must give them content that resonates with them. So, how can you do this? By finding out what your audience struggles, challenges, goals, or needs are; it's the best way to connect and engage. This enables you to provide the value they need so you can get them the results they want. Ask questions and listen to the feedback they give; this lets you know you're on the right track. Don't stop there. Determine whether your content is getting them results. Determine the best way to provide the right solutions for them. It's so much easier to connect when you don't put most of your emphasis on sales. There's nothing wrong with wanting to make sales.

However, you certainly don't want to be pushy or "salesy". Can you imagine going to a website and seeing nothing but 'Add to Cart' and 'Buy Now' buttons all over each page? It's important to genuinely connect with your potential clients or customers. You want to be able to serve them in the best possible way.

Here's the winning formula to achieve it:

1. Discover their needs and wants

2. Demonstrate that you understand their needs

3. Show them how you're able to provide a solution with your product

4. Then you can invite them to buy from you

Knowing that you provide something that people not only find value in, but gets results, will certainly keep you motivated. You'll have the encouragement you need to keep going, despite the roadblocks or setbacks you might face along your road to success.

8 Master Your Time

Your time is precious. Due to life's daily demands, it can seem as if there's not enough left to focus on the things that matter to you. Building your online business is important to you. It's absolutely necessary to manage your time in such a way that allows you to be fully engaged with your online business, yet maintain balance in your life. Your online success depends on how well you manage your time. The moment you designate time to building your business, you are strategically aligning yourself with your purpose. This empowers you to achieve your biggest goals. As you manage your time, you become the one in the driver's seat. People and things that have stolen your time in the past can no longer interfere with your progress. You'll have the freedom to take the necessary steps to build your digital empire.

Priority Leads to Prosperity

You may feel as though there's not enough time in a day to complete your daily task to build your business. However, by focusing on the right tasks, you'll get closer to your dreams in no time. The key to doing this is prioritizing business related task. Learn to command your day. Each night before bed make a list of 3 to 5 task or steps you can take the next day to complete. Designate a certain amount of time each day that you can invest in your business; even if you only start with 30 minutes to an hour. At some point, you will be able to do more because time flies while you're pursuing your passion.

So, if you're having an issue finding the time, then this will help you create it! So, don't be afraid to start small with the time you have; even if it's a small time frame. As you begin to see all the progress you make each day, you'll experience real results. Before you know it, your online business will begin to generate income.

The top 3 things you can do immediately to prioritize your business:

1. **Deal with Interference:** Learn how to effectively deal with people and things that interfere with your goals and time. Sometimes people will divert your attention from your business. Some may not realize it, and then there are others who do it deliberately. These are the ones you'll need to set strong boundaries with.

2. **Deal with Procrastination:** In order to master your time, you must effectively deal with procrastination. Putting off your business task will only cause you unnecessary stress and frustration. The simplest method for dealing with procrastination is to start! Simply dive into the parts of your tasks that excite you the most. Break down larger

aspects of your business projects into micro-steps.

3. **Stay Organized:** Keep yourself and your work area organized. When you are organized, you give yourself the freedom to think and act freely. This frees your mind to focus on the most important aspects of your business. It also gives you the freedom to create and make the best decisions for your business.

Find Your Hustle Zone

Part of being productive is having a special area where you can get in the zone and get things done. I call this the Hustle Zone. If you're going to effectively master your time, you'll need to have a space where you can easily focus on things related to your online business. It's great if you can designate a room for this. However, if you don't have a separate room for your space, clear an area in a quiet room that's free from distractions. Once you create your Hustle Zone, set it up in such a way that will help you be the most productive. Be sure to let others know this will be your space for work. Set some boundaries and let them know you are not to be disturbed while in your Hustle Zone.

What if it's nearly impossible or at the very least a little difficult to have your own 'Hustle Zone'? This may be due to a living situation. Simple, find a space somewhere else where you can get your work done. You can find a spot at a local restaurant, coffee shop, a library, park, or a co-working space.

Whether it's in your home or somewhere else, find a place that works for you.

Self-Mastery

Mastering your time in your online business assists you in daily decision making and helps grow your business. It becomes so much easier to keep yourself on track through technology. There are tons of apps and programs that can help you make the most of your time and be productive. It's important for up and coming digital marketers to master their time because many work full-time jobs while building their business in their down time. As you take this journey, it's important to find the right tools for you that will help with productivity and organization.

Here are a few apps that I love:

- Evernote
- Tasks: To-Do list
- WinGo Plan
- Dropbox
- Mindly
- Timecap

Another important aspect of being productive is making sure you have time for yourself to simply relax and recharge. Your business is nothing unless you take care of yourself. I'm always happy to see aspiring entrepreneurs hustling and putting in the work. However, you don't need to allow yourself to become burnt out. It's hard to provide value to your audience when your energy level is low. In addition, it takes away from your power of focus; zapping your creativity and drive. You can't pour from an empty cup. Be sure to make time for yourself to do things you enjoy outside of your work; balance is key!

Finally, the biggest enemy to being productive is resistance. The most common things I have found amongst new digital marketers are, "not feeling like it" or feeling "bored". Ever have a task or project that you really needed to work on, but just couldn't bring yourself to do it? Boredom or not feeling like it is a form of resistance. It typically comes from frustration or uncertainty on a particular aspect of the project you're working on. Sometimes, it's only a perceived issue, like the pesky 'what if' scenarios that we create in our own mind. Other times it's a decision that needs to be made that we're reluctant to make.

> **"**
> Be confident in your decisions and stick with them long enough to see what works and what doesn't.

Avoidance creates a self-imposed road-block that can only set you back even further. How do you overcome this? Easy...start! Once you start, keep going, and take consistent action. Be confident in your decisions and stick with them long enough to see what works and what doesn't work. Success comes to those who effectively master their time.

9 Digital Marketing Blueprint

Now that you know you only need to 'start' so you can be productive in your digital business; it's time to figure out where to start. For many aspiring digital marketers taking the first steps and knowing where to start can seem a bit complicated or over-whelming. That's why it's important to have a rock-solid system to follow. In many ways, being creative in your business is great, but there are certain things you simply don't have to reinvent. This is where some new marketers get stuck. The lack of having a system in place often makes the easiest aspects of your business ten times harder.

Having the right system to follow can bring you digital marketing success if you follow it properly. Your plan or blueprint will help you figure out what really works for your business.

> **"**
> Taking a focused approach let's you tune into what your list really wants so you can offer products & services they love.

In a moment I'll show you what's needed for a powerful system, but first I need to explain why the lack of a system can kill your business. Digital marketing requires you to build an email list. You must be able to engage with your audience on this level. You can buy an email list, but your business can only thrive if you build your own list of people you know are actually interested in your content and want to buy from you. So it's important for you to learn how to build a highly responsive email list.

Taking a focused approach lets you tune into what your list really wants so you can offer products or services they love. Your email list is a group of people who find value in your content and can become a potential customer. The lack of a system could keep you from turning these leads into buyers. A good system requires you to follow up on your customers. Doing so will allow them to progress in their goal while you present to them the right tools and resources for their

success. This can mean the difference between a one-time customer and a community
of people who are repeat buyers.

Method Mastery

There are many online business models
that can provide passive income. Choosing
the right business model to start with can
give you the freedom you desire. Three of the
easiest ones you can get started with immediately are blogs, Instagram theme pages,
and affiliate marketing. All of these business
models are very rewarding. Some digital
marketers combine a few methods to help
them maximize their earnings. I'm sure
you've visited popular blogs in your online
searches. Maybe you've even wondered about

starting your own. You can utilize it to deliver content on a regular basis that people are searching for daily. Affiliate marketing is simply recommending a product to others and earning a commission for it when they purchase it. When you use both of these methods (if you choose to) together, you can build an audience of sub-scribers and loyal fans who enjoy your content and buy from you. It's a profitable system that can help you earn.

As you've learned, the lack of a system is one of the biggest obstacles for aspiring digital marketers. Your system simplifies the process for you and your customers. Now there's a ton of different systems out there for digital marketing. However, there's an easy to follow formula that I've used from day one that works well.

Step 1: Your Product

It doesn't matter if it's a creation of your own or a product that you offer as an affiliate, it's essential to understand exactly what you're offering. You must understand the core purpose of your product. Amongst new marketers the easiest and quickest way to make real money online is selling other people's products as an affiliate. You could earn money and build a thriving online business selling things like courses, coaching programs, software, or even services while making passive income. When promoting products for others it's essential to know all you can about it.

· What's the purpose of it?

· Is it relevant?

· Is there a demand for it?

· Are others selling this or something like it?

These are some of the factors you'll need to consider when choosing an affiliate offer.

Step 2: Your Target Audience

Now that you've found a product to promote and you understand it fully, you need to find the demographic of people who would most likely buy your product. In order to meet the needs of your audience you'll need to understand them better. Get to know them, their age, gender, likes/dislikes, location, and interest. Having this information will allow you to help them with the right solution.

Step 3: Your Marketing Method

Once you've been able to pinpoint who your target audience is, you'll need to uncover your marketing method. There are plenty of methods, but the key is to find what's right for you. Maybe a certain combination of different methods can work for you? It absolutely could! Simply start with one and then branch out to others.

What are some of these methods? Here are just a few: blogging, search engine optimization, email marketing, video marketing, and social medial marketing to name a few. Utilizing these methods can connect you to your audience. You don't have to be an expert in all of these areas at once. Learn and test things out as you go. This is the only way to find what works with your audience and your products.

Success Starts Now

Why would you choose to make passive income through affiliate marketing instead of creating your own product as a complete beginner? You don't have to deal with the lengthy process of product creation. It takes a good amount of time to create a digital product from scratch. Affiliate marketing gives you an opportunity to find the right niche for you, an easy way to learn the internet marketing process, and a faster path to earning money online. As you earn this passive income you're gaining the freedom you desire and the fulfillment of building a business you love. Not to mention the fact that you can choose a product that is already selling well. You simply need to find the best method of promoting it that works for you. Affiliate marketing is one of the simplest and low-risk ways to build a digital empire in your free time. You can start as a side hustle, and if you choose, make it a fulltime business that replaces your job. In the next chapter, I'll demonstrate how everything you've learned so far works together. Then I'll show you the actions you can take to make your digital empire a reality.

10 Hustle & Grow

When you believe in yourself, and over-come limiting beliefs like fear, doubt, and negative thoughts; that's the biggest step to success you can take in your digital business. Too many people set themselves up for defeat because they never took the time to overcome these obstacles before trying to build their empire. They have trouble gaining any traction and give up before they create any results. They allow themselves to be-come discouraged. Throughout this book you've been given the keys to deal with these common roadblocks.

You've literally taken the initiative that most people wouldn't. You've set yourself up for continued success. Many people read books about digital marketing, gain lots of knowledge, love what they learn, but never take action on it. You have set yourself apart from the wantrepreneurs.

The Art of Hustle

Hustle is all about being consistent and following through on your goals. It's one thing to talk about success or simply share quotes on Instagram; it's another thing to actually take the steps to be successful. The only way to reach your goals is to put in the work. You're going to have to put in the time to get there. So often, the people who seem to be an overnight success have been putting in the work behind the scenes for a while, sometimes years. Before you know it, the time you put in pays off.

> **❝**
> Be hungry for knowledge that
> you can take action upon
> so you can build a
> thriving business you love.

One of the most important aspects of your hustle is the need to stay hungry. The world of digital marketing and online business in general is ever changing. It's a must that you build a solid foundation to grow your business. Be hungry for knowledge that you can take action upon so you can build a thriving business you love. What are the key actions you must take to build your business?

Here's a list of the Hustle Moves you must make to generate real income online:

6 Hustle Moves for Digital Marketers

· Clarify your vision and marketing message

· Employ Mindset Mastery to overcome your biggest challenges

· Identify your niche and ideal audience

· Create outstanding content that engages your audience and monetize it

· Create offers for your products that bring in leads and sales

· Build an email list of people who enjoy your content

In just a moment I'll show you how to make these Hustle Moves work for you, but before I do, there's a few more important things you need to know so you can unlock the power of these strategies.

Action is everything in your digital business. Many people who have a desire to start an online business may believe it only takes minimal effort or have been sold the idea of 'no real work and instant riches' by less than honest gurus. Here's the truth... the key to building a real, thriving business online requires commitment and real effort. Does this business model give you the ability to make passive or semi-passive income? Yes. However, for this to take place, you must be willing to take action, and put in the work upfront to build a solid system that makes you money.

The next important factor to know is that the best ideas are worthless without action. You may have something brilliant to offer, but nobody will ever discover what you have to offer unless you take action. Once you find the right niche for you, start small. Get out there and test it. Be sure to invest a reasonable amount of time consistently promoting your offer and measuring your results. Finally, don't allow yourself to fall into the trap of half-finished projects. Success mastery is all about building a thriving online business that you love. The only way to do that is by following through on your goals. The fact that you are reading this book shows that you have what it takes. You are fully capable of achieving success online.

First Steps

I want to show you this step-by-step overview of the immediate action steps you can take now for online success.

· Recognize how important your mindset is. Remember, you have the power to change your mindset every day.

· Harness your strengths. Recognize how valuable your skills are and the things you can do to continue learning and building them.

· Understand that what you see as failure or mistakes, are only a lesson on what does and doesn't work. You control your perception.

· Focus on the value that you have to offer. Drown out the words of naysayers.

As you've seen, the purpose of this book is to help you take the first steps toward online business success. You've learned how to overcome challenges that stop most people in their tracks. You've learned the primary factors that mean the difference between the average person and successful digital entrepreneurs. I promised you earlier that I'll show you how to make the '6 Hustle Moves' work for you. I want to invite you to join me for some free training on starting your online business. Take action now! Get in on this free training and I'll show you what it takes to start your digital marketing journey.

About the Author

E. Renee Williams is a Digital Marketing Consultant, Certified Success Coach, and Author. Over the last 9 years, Renee has become the trusted success and marketing expert to digital entrepreneurs and small business owners.

With outstanding experience in digital marketing strategies, course creation, sales funnels, list building and personal development, Renee provides a unique combination of powerful marketing and success strategies that have proven to get massive results. Renee's value lies in her unique ability to help her clients build and grow a thriving online business.

Free Online Business Success Training

As a special thank you for purchasing a copy of Success Mastery, I want to give you free access to my success training program for new digital entrepreneurs.

It's called…'The Way 2 Victory'.

This is a special 4 part video training that I created with aspiring digital entrepreneurs in mind. **Go to the website below or scan the QR code.**

SuccessMasteryBook.com/free-training

Notes